Good Morning,
Baiting Hollow!

Written by Patricia Clark Smith

Paintings by Barbara A. Clark, ED.D.

8/15/15

www.trafford.com

North America & international
toll-free: 1 888 232 4444 (USA & Canada)
fax: 812 355 4082

Good Morning, Baiting Hollow!

Good Morning Baiting Hollow
by Patricia Clark Smith

↓ Poem by Patricia Clark Smith...
↓ Paintings by Barbara Clark

©2013

Dedicated to: *Maggie and Barbara*

Good Morning, Baiting Hollow!

First light, crack of dawn,
Golden edged clouds in the eastern sky,
Tiny bungalows bathed in soft pink light,
A sleepy little beach awakens.

A seagull screeches and flies from his cliff home,
Other gulls called to the beach, follow.
Their attention, now facing the new sunrise,
They salute, "Good morning, Baiting Hollow!"

Dragonflies heed the herald's call,
With sparrows, terns, and piping plovers,
Leaving their safe snug marsh homes,
To feast on insects, mussels, and minnows.

Stepping out onto our mercottage deck,
With warm cups of coffee, to meet the new day.
We take in deep breaths of the clean salt air
And survey the sky and waters with care.

Puffy white clouds float in clear blue sky,
As white caps dance on top of waves,
A sailboat or two glide across the horizon,
And terns dive into the cold salt water.

Like giant angels, the great cliffs
Silently stand guard this small beach hollow,
There to watch over, protect, and preserve,
Now, as in days gone by.

A trawler's chugging, way out at sea,
Breaks the quiet of Baiting Hollow and its menagerie.
The fishermen and lobstermen launching their boats,
Set out for a deep sea harvest with high hopes.

A beach comber arrives at the water's edge,
Strolling and searching Baiting Hollow sand
For treasures of sea glass, shells, stones, and more
Washed up in waves and left on the shore.

By midmorning, umbrellas, blankets, and toys
Are strewn here and there for visitors to enjoy.
Sun bathers, jet skiers, those swimming or reading,
All came to Baiting Hollow to relax and have fun.

When the sun is high and the mermaids sleep,
We retreat to the bungalow for shelter and rest.
Lazy afternoons, stories, memories, and laughter,
Join family and friends in time ever after.

Every evening beach people sit on the sand by the sea.

Sunset is a masterpiece, all would agree.

Then the quiet, the peace of a star filled night sky,

Reflections of God's glory, a sacred blessing,

We sigh...

" At Sunset We'll
Sing ... "

Day is done. Gone the sun.
From the lakes, from the hills,
From the sky.
All is well, safely rest.

God is Nigh !!

"... Just take it as it comes..."

M. Edwards July, 2012

Thank you Pat,
Love,
Barbara
xo

Printed in the United States
by Baker & Taylor Publisher Services